MONSTER MANNERS

At Mealtimes

Written by
Charis Mather

Designed by
Amy Li

American adaptation copyright © 2026 by North Star Editions, Mendota Heights, MN 55120. All rights reserved. No part of this book may be reproduced or utilized in any form or by any means without written permission from the publisher.

At Mealtimes © 2024 BookLife Publishing
This edition is published by arrangement with BookLife Publishing

Library of Congress Control Number:
2024953063

ISBN
979-8-89359-329-7 (library bound)
979-8-89359-413-3 (paperback)
979-8-89359-384-6 (epub)
979-8-89359-359-4 (hosted ebook)

Printed in the United States of America
Mankato, MN
092025

sales@northstareditions.com
888-417-0195

Written by:
Charis Mather

Edited by:
Rebecca Phillips-Bartlett

Designed by:
Amy Li

All facts, statistics, web addresses and URLs in this book were verified as valid and accurate at time of writing. No responsibility for any changes to external websites or references can be accepted by either the author or publisher.

PHOTO CREDITS
All images are courtesy of Shutterstock.com, unless otherwise specified. With thanks to Getty Images, ThinkStock Photo and iStockphoto.

Recurring — Agafonov Oleg, Archiwiz, Curly Pat, Omeris, Dedraw Studio. P3 — natchapohn. P8 — Line-of-thought.

Monsters know many things.

They know how to cook and how to clean...

They know how to go shopping and how to look after pets...

But there is one thing that many monsters do not know...

MANNERS!

Tickles and Pod were excited. Tonight, Gram Gram was coming to visit while Mama and Papa were out. Gram Gram always made the best meals. Tickles licked her lips.

Thinking about Gram Gram's food made Tickles's tummy rumble. The funny noise made her little brother laugh. Then his tummy rumbled, too!

The monsters giggled. Then they heard a knock at the door.

"Did I hear a pair of grumbling tummies?" said a familiar voice.

An older monster poked her head into the room. "It must be nearly dinnertime."

"Gram Gram!" the little monsters squealed.

Tickles and Pod gave Gram Gram a big hug.

"Gram Gram, we were just thinking about your cooking," Tickles said. "You make the best mashed potatoes."

"Make us some mashed potatoes!" Pod said.

"Yes," said Tickles. "A giant bowl of mashed potatoes, as big as me!"

"We couldn't possibly eat that much mashed potatoes on our own," said Gram Gram.

"Mama and Papa can help us eat it," Pod said.

"We could set up a fancy meal for when they get back," Tickles suggested.

"That's a great idea," said Gram Gram. "But you will have to learn some mealtime manners first."

"Make sure to use soap!" Gram Gram called after them. Meanwhile, Gram Gram filled the teapot and put out the little plates, cups, and saucers. Then the children came back.

"Let's see those hands," Gram Gram said.

Pod and Tickles wiggled their clean fingers and giggled. Gram Gram smiled. "Wonderful. Now we are ready to eat."

Just then, Tickles's phone pinged. She checked her messages. "Look, Pod. Addy sent me a photo of her pet. He's so cute!"

"Tickles, please could you put that away while we eat?" Gram Gram said. "Monsters with good manners don't use their phones at the table."

Bloop!

"Of course, Gram Gram," said Tickles.

Gram Gram smiled and passed Tickles and Pod their teacups. "Thank you, Tickles. Not using your phone is a good way to show respect for the people you are eating with."

Tickles put her phone away. Then Pod reached over the table. He put all three muffins on his own plate.

"Pod, please could you share those muffins with us?" said Gram Gram. "Monsters with good manners make sure that everyone at the table gets a fair amount of food."

Tickles took a big mouthful of muffin. "Mm, mm, mm," she said. "Monster muffins are delicious." As Tickles spoke, little pieces of muffin sprayed out of her mouth. Some crumbs landed on Pod.

"Ew!" said Pod, laughing. He spat a mouthful of crumbs back at his sister.

"FOOD FIGHT!" Tickles yelled.

She reached for more food to fling at Pod.

Quickly, Gram Gram moved the food out of their reach. "What a mess! Monsters with good manners do not play with their food."

"Oh," said the kids through mouthfuls of muffin crumbs. They looked at the table. "That did make quite a big mess. We should clean that up," Tickles said.

"That is a great idea," Gram Gram agreed. "Monsters with manners often offer to help out at mealtimes."

Together, Pod and Tickles cleaned up the crumbs. "Thank you, kids," Gram Gram said. "Let's pause our lessons on manners for now. Mama and Papa won't be long. I've got mashed potatoes to make."

"Yay!" the kids shouted.

Pod was right. Mama and Papa were very surprised. Pod and Tickles ran off to wash their hands and put their phones away.

They were even more surprised when Pod offered to help Gram Gram dish out a fair amount of mashed potatoes to everyone at the table.

But Mama and Papa were most surprised when Pod and Tickles did not start a food fight during the meal.

"You really have learned your manners," Mama said, proud of her well-behaved little monsters.

"Not even one bit of mashed potatoes thrown," Papa said, amazed.

Tickles and Pod nodded. "Gram Gram taught us that food fights make a big mess," Tickles said.

"Well, what are we supposed to do with all of these leftover mashed potatoes now?" Papa wondered.

Tickles had an idea.

"I know someone who might have a better use for these leftovers than a food fight. Gram Gram, please may I send a message on my phone?"

"Just this once," Gram Gram agreed. "Thank you for checking with me first."

Quickly, Tickles sent out a message.

Not long later, there was a knock at the door. It was Addy and her lovely little pet.

Addy's pet smelled the delicious mashed potatoes right away. Before anyone could stop him, he jumped up onto the dinner table, right into the big bowl of leftovers!

Mashed potatoes went everywhere!

Not all monsters have good manners, but Tickles and Pod do. Do you?

Can you remember Gram Gram's mealtime manners?

- Wash your hands before eating.
- Put away your phones.
- Be fair when sharing food.
- Be helpful.
- Absolutely no playing with your food—if you can help it!